Inkspiration

A Collection of Poetic Musings

Aishwarya Damodar

Made with ❤ on the Notion Press Platform

www.notionpress.com

Dedication

In cherished memory of my late father, whose abiding presence serves as a guiding light to me. This book stands as a heartfelt tribute to the man who held unshakable faith in my abilities.

His boundless love and enduring care have left an indelible mark on my journey, forever influencing its trajectory.

Acknowledgements

I would like to express my heartfelt appreciation to the following individuals whose invaluable roles have given fruition to my poetry.

To my beloved mother, Bhakti whose presence has been a source of unwavering support and whose encouragement has been a wellspring of inspiration, guiding me through the intricate maze of this creative expedition.

To all my teachers from my Alma Mater, for imparting invaluable lessons in language and poetry.

To Nitin Thakker, my guardian angel, whose belief in both me and my work has rendered the publication of this book a reality.

To Joy Becker, whose camaraderie and thoughtful insights brought exhilaration and creativity during the writing process.

To Sudha Shenoy Pai, the steadfast pillar by my side; whose support and solidarity have offered solace and strength through every chapter of my life.

To Shilpa Agnihotri, whose knack for meaningful foreign phrases stimulated and sparked a few poems in this collection.

To my brother, Akshay, whose quizzical expressions and varied responses to my poems, reminded me of the diverse ways we perceive life.

To Nitya Chama Rao, whose affability and interpretations continually inspired this literary odyssey.

Your contributions have brought this book to life, and for that, I am profoundly grateful.

Thank You!

Contents

NATURE

INSPIRATIONAL

EXPLORATION OF MIND

NATURE

Poems celebrating the beauty, wonder and interconnectedness of the natural world.

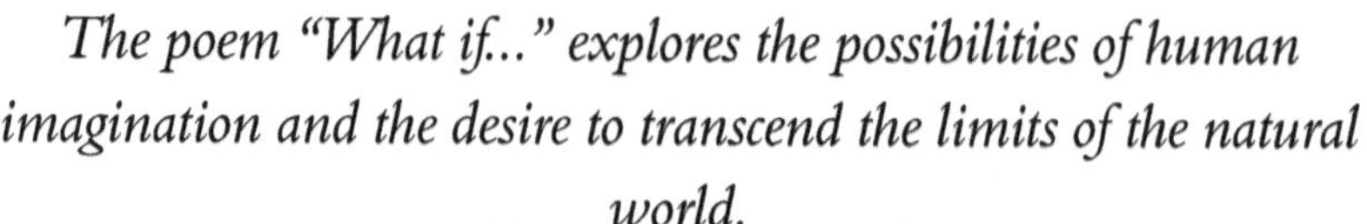

The poem "What if..." explores the possibilities of human imagination and the desire to transcend the limits of the natural world.

What If...

What if...

What if we could reach the sky?

feel the warmth of the sun

fly amongst the stars and planets

who seem so near and yet so far.

What if...

What if we could walk on sea?

speak the language of the oceans

sway against the wind with the trees

hear the flowers whisper words

as they flutter their petals in the breeze.

What if...

What if we could rage a storm?

bellow back our angry cry,

flash the lightening smitten bolts,

strike the mighty world from the sky.

What if...

What if we could be the earth?

be in oneness with nature grandeur

swing in harmony with every mother's song

keep only goodness and blow away every wrong.

What if...

What if we could fly away?

to horizons unknown, destinations anew,

blend with the sea, embrace the starry sky,

Oh, what if...we could fly?

The poem "Beyond the Veil" is a captivating exploration of a hidden world where secrets dance, mysteries await discovery, and imagination knows no bounds.

Beyond the Veil

Beyond the veil, a hidden world lies,

where secrets dance beneath starlit skies,

mysteries untold, waiting to be found,

in the realms where imagination knows no bounds.

Beyond the veil, where fantasy resides,

where the ordinary fades and wonder presides,

through nature's fabric, we venture deep,

where mystical souls, their secrets keep.

Beyond the veil, a symphony of desires,

where passion ignites and the heart inspires,

the brush of a breeze, a gentle caress,

unleashing enchantment, unleashing finesse.

Beyond the veil, where the impossible gleams,

where the limits of reality burst at the seams,

in the domain of possibilities, we find our release,

a sanctuary for the soul, a place of inner peace.

Let us journey together, hand in hand,

into the spheres where dreams expand,

beyond the veil, let our spirits unfurl,

and discover the magic that resides in our world.

The poem "Celestial Reverie" describes the poet's desire to escape the daily grind and find solace in the beauty of the clouds.

Celestial Reverie

Tired of the hard day that I left behind,
I sat through my journey with a hazy mind,
I wanted to drift away from the day-to-day grind,
when my sights got arrested by the cloudy bind.

Echoing silence from the bluish white isle,
a visual treat that few brushes could style,
O! What a difference from the chaotic earth,
translucent effervescence floating in mirth.

Sun setting beneath rushes of rain swept clouds,
moon standing tall aside wavelets of river troughs,
realm of universe in this cloud lined comb,
relaxed like a child in a mother's womb.

Dancing and galloping and flying,
drifting enroute and re-joining,
sparkling in dusky glow so lustrous,
singing a song in a tone so wondrous
creating a powerful melody that strung in harmony,
unparalleled on Planet Earth.

The poem "Forever Oneness with Nature" celebrates the author's escape to the embrace of nature and the deep connection she feels with its beauty and tranquility.

Forever Oneness with Nature

Seeking solace from the concrete jungle's grip,

amidst Nature's embrace, I find my spirit's trip.

Colors, melodies and landscapes untamed,

renewing my soul, leaving me unchained.

From meadows to rivers, nature's endless flow,

teaching resilience, the wisdom I bestow.

In secluded spots, I find solace and peace,

healing within, my inner conflicts cease.

Though my time is fleeting, the connection remains,

Nature's power, forever in my veins.

A sacred bond, beyond words can express,

Oneness with Nature, my eternal address.

INSPIRATIONAL

Poems that uplift and motivate, offering encouragement and strength.

The poem "HOPE" is about the difficulties of life and the power of hope to guide us through them.

Hope

Anarchic is the world

in which we live-in today

where money has become the master, and

we are its bonded slaves

where hurts of our past

have made their homes in our heart

where fears of tepid future

has left us frenzied, groping in the dark.

Though the journey seems intriguing

do not succumb to the testing times

in the end, all will be right

just keep looking for the light

it's the rule of the universe

that after every dusk comes the dawn

the darkest hours in our lives

can only last until the morn.

When you feel, you are done and dusted with life,

hold onto HOPE to guide you through such strife.

When the paths seem steep and hard to climb,

HOPE is the balm that will soothe your mind.

When trials seem unrelenting and shatter your soul,

HOPE is the sparkle that will make you feel whole.

When tears stream silently down your eyes,

in such faces of travesty is where HOPE abides.

———❀❀———

The poem "Sunfire Journey" captures the essence of achieving by embracing challenges and hardships, akin to the Sun's fiery journey.

———❀❀———

Sunfire Journey

If you aspire to radiate like the Sun's light,
you must endure the flames and burn bright,
for breaking boundaries and making your mark,
requires strength and a fiery spark.

Set your vision wide, push yourself beyond,
transform dreams into reality, resolute and strong,
embrace nature's wisdom, learn and obey,
grasp life's nuances on your journey's way.

Remember, nothing comes without a cost,
effort and sacrifice are never lost,
to shine like the Sun, luminous and grand,
first, embrace the flames and take a stand.

The poem "Life's Voyage" revolves around the metaphor of life as a voyage filled with experiences and discoveries.

Life's Voyage

As you traverse life's winding road,

amidst fellow sojourners and challenges bestowed,

fear not when crossroads arise,

for beyond them, a new dawn lies.

Choose your path with a tranquil mind,

embrace life's ebbs and flows you find,

retreat if needed, but return with might,

unlearn, learn, and grow in the light.

Nature's mysteries shall invigorate,

time as your mentor, guiding your fate,

absorb life's nuances, both subtle and grand,

forge ahead toward dreams that expand.

At the destination, find bliss and pride,

a testament to the journey's stride,

for in the end, your story will be told,

a life well-traveled, worth more than gold.

The poem "Ichi-go Ichi-e" reflects on the transformative impact of a pandemic, reminding us to appreciate the present moment and live it fully, as each moment is unique and cannot be recreated.

Ichi-go Ichi-e

a virus

a pandemic

did the unthinkable

they got us on our knees

mopped our cobwebbed minds

cleared our vision

recalibrated our goals

and showed us

what really mattered

in our lives

and what did not

the bliss of breathing free,

the joy in little things,

the wonders of living healthy,

the love of friends and family.

ichi-go ichi-e

no moment can be recreated

live it fully

The poem "Et sic incipit..." reflects on the challenges faced in the year following the COVID outbreak, while embracing a new normal with hope, belief, and the determination to move forward.

Et Sic Incipit...

after a year of stress

we ended with a strain

the carefree life we once lived

we will never find it again

the year seemed long, but

it left us strong

through every hit and fall

we emerged out tall

the normal way of living

had to be redefined

a new normal has now been

ingrained in our mind

we no longer fear

practicality is our gear

the statistics are only numbers

they no more rip us asunder

with hope as our armor, and

belief restored

we move in confident strides

having faith in the guiding light.

et sic incipit

and, so it begins...

The poem "By Faith..." expresses the belief in the power of faith to navigate through life's challenges, find hope, and trust in a higher guiding force.

By Faith...

by faith, I believe

that faith is choosing to believe

that the journey of life is meant to be, the way it is.

by faith, I believe

that eventually things will fall in place

that there is HOPE always and this truth cannot be displaced.

by faith, I believe

that when life's valleys seem mired and dark

there will be a conduit out there that will take me out.

by faith, I believe

that I am not alone

that there is an angel up there watching my every move.

by faith, I believe

that when the time is ripe

the Universe will conspire to reveal what is right.

by faith, I believe

that it is in *faith* that I have to BELIEVE

to move on in Life.

The poem "The game is set..." portrays the journey of a ravaged heart longing to be heard and ready to face the challenges of life.

The Game is Set...

a ravaged heart

beautiful and violent

engulfed in a raging fire

pining, craving and longing

for her elegy to be heard

but there is no one around

the game is set, but

she is not ready...

she has to fight

the fears gripping her

the demons tormenting her

weave the torn fabric

heal the scalds, while

letting the scars be

the game is set, now

she is poised...

to take controls

fortified with faith

armed with hope

her heart is ready

ready to blossom

ready to fly

ready to face

the challenges of life

the game is set, and

so is she

The poem "BE YOU" encourages resilience and self-belief in the face of tough times.

Be You

Tough times come

tough times go

just like

how the seasons do

stop not

do not succumb

even when the travails

hit you low.

Stumbling blocks

will pave way

to clear paths

Universe will guide

you through

bestowing you with signs

guiding you to a world

that is waiting for you.

BElieve in **YOU**rself

BE YOU.

The poem "We make a difference." emphasizes the significance of individual contributions in fulfilling our purpose and collectively shaping the world, drawing parallels to the interconnectedness found in nature's elements.

We Make a Difference.

Within every soul, a spark resides,
a power within that subtly guides,
through actions big and small, we see,
how each one shapes our destiny.

Imagine if a single drop of rain,
believed its fall was in vain,
but together, they create rivers wide,
and nourish the earth, far and wide.

What if a solitary seed thought,
its growth and bloom would matter naught,
yet forests emerge from a humble start,
as each seed plays its vital part.

In a symphony, each note's embrace,
contributes to the melody's grace,
a single voice, though small in sound,
blends with others, harmonies resound.

Remember, in life's grand design,

every life is intertwined,

with every step and choice we make,

the world transforms, for our sake.

So let us embrace our unique role,

for within us lies a precious soul,

with love, compassion, and persistence,

together, we make a world of difference.

EXPLORATION OF MIND

*Poems that explore the depths of thoughts, emotions, and
the complexities of the human mind.*

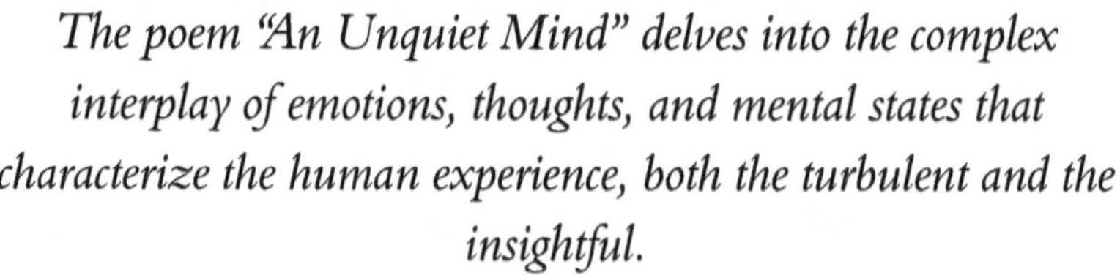

The poem "An Unquiet Mind" delves into the complex interplay of emotions, thoughts, and mental states that characterize the human experience, both the turbulent and the insightful.

An Unquiet Mind

An unquiet mind

is of the salient kind

trapped in

melancholy

mania and asinine

ballistic efforts

juxtaposed with

malignant thoughts, and

unchecked exuberance

causing skepticism

troubled dreams, and

fallible endeavors

forever drowning in

faded eclectic lines.

In the flashing

revelations of

the mind's

wonderful fire

also lie the

sky borne ideas

triggered from an

astringent intellect

creating a plausible

enterprise with

frenzied enthusiasm

and gravitas.

Every fury, pain

qualm and joy

every high, low

mood and sigh

that can be

felt with certainty

by the inner

conscience

of a human soul

lie within the expanse

of this very

unquiet mind.

The poem "Remember" explores the concept of memories that have been unseen and unfelt for a long time, yet resurface through various triggers such as songs, pictures, words, and fleeting moments.

Remember

Unseen

Unfelt

from time out of mind

auld lang syne

a song here

a picture there

a word spoken

a memory in motion

tugs it out

from the wedges

incised deeply

over the years.

cryptic

enigmatic

prejudicial

mysterial

faded from seasons

threadbare sublime

detached diffident strains

Yet. Somehow. It remains.

Remember?

The poem "Enlivened" portrays the journey from turmoil to clarity, highlighting the importance of faith and introspection in restoring inner vitality and finding solace in one's soul.

Enlivened

the set of events

that unfolded

had triggered

the unwarranted

first...

she lost her sleep, and

then the tears

eventually, the edginess

and turmoil took over.

it took the quietness, and

nothingness

of several nights

to set things clear

in lucid light

faith restored

reignited her spark

it enlivened her soul

it enlivened her heart.

The poem "Nostalgia" reflects on the contemplative moments of
the present and the memories of the past.

Nostalgia

here I am

and, there

wondering...

over the moments of yonder

intersected in mind

that bring back memories

some making sense

some irrelevant

learnings, unlearnt

that were relearnt

as the journey

stumbled through

it's twists and turns

as new souls connected

and, loved ones died

emotions crocheted

into a beguiled mesh

creating a mystical story

of a heart and mind

that has bled with tears

blossomed in love, and

basked in the glory of the light

here I am

and, there...

EXISTENTIAL

Contemplative poems that explore the meaning of life, existence, and the mysteries of our existence.

The poem "Time flies by..." reminds us not to postpone meaningful connections and relationships, emphasizing the swift passage of time and the need to prioritize caring for others before it's too late.

Time Flies By...

There is a saying that goes

While we are postponing

life speeds by...

In our quest

to fulfill our dreams

we tend to focus

only on the mainstream

forgetting all the relations

that we made along the way

not bothering to make that call

or write that mail

to check about their well-being

to know that they are fine

we keep saying to ourselves

that soon we will find that time.

But, time and tide wait for no man.

The distraught flickering souls
who waited for us in despair
hoping that someday
we would find the time to spare
are one fine day mortalized
even before we realize
the importance of how much
they needed us in their lives.

So, walk that extra mile, and
give that friendly smile
profess how much you love
express how much you care
for there is wisdom in the saying
this ain't a lie -
While you keep postponing
Time flies by...
Yes. Time flies by.
le temps passe vite

The poem "Music for every Soul" celebrates the power of music to touch and evoke various emotions within us.

Music for every Soul

a soulful rendition

a plaintive melody

a melancholy

intense, light, heavy,

romantic, blue,

there are so many moods

that soothe you

heal you

make you groove,

sensitizing every feeling

be it happiness, sadness,

emptiness,

passion or love,

there is always a chord

that resonates within you

riveting, gripping,

expressing,

where words fail

reflecting

what you are going through.

Dance with the rhythm

let the music flow

there is music for you

there is music for me

there is music for every soul.

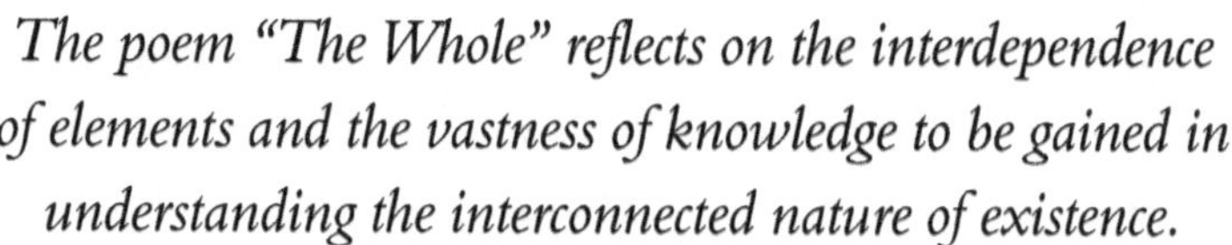

*The poem "The Whole" reflects on the interdependence
of elements and the vastness of knowledge to be gained in
understanding the interconnected nature of existence.*

The Whole

We wander outside

in quest of the whole

we delve inside

to find the whole.

When the time is ripe for us

to comprehend and grow

we realize

that it is from the whole

that the whole is materialized.

There is more to understand

there is more to learn

about the mystical power

that designs the domains

even after the whole

is taken out from the whole

the whole still remains

complete and diverse.

The poem "Black O' White" explores the symbolic meaning of black and white and how they represent contrasting aspects of life.

Black O' White

A tabula rasa canvas

of pure white

heralding new beginnings

gets interspersed

with stark silhouettes

drawn in black

as we move on

with the rhythm of life.

While white reflects fullness

black reflects emptiness

both exemplify the extremes

of the dispersion of colors

as they move through the prism

in tandem with the path

we traverse from life to death

tracing the contours of our breath.

The poem "Fragmented" delves into the intricate landscape of a mind filled with fragmented thoughts and emotions.

Fragmented

fragmented mind filled with

fragmented thoughts

fragmented feelings in a

fragmented heart

fragmented darkness streaked with

fragmented white

O! what do I make of this

fragmented life?

The poem "UnBelonged" delves into the inner turmoil of a person who feels disconnected and out of place, grappling with conflicting emotions and a sense of not belonging.

UnBelonged

disconnected within

she did not know

whether

she was fighting it all

or giving-in

to the warped time

that had shrouded

her powerless, emotionless

she did not know

whether

it should have mattered at all

or have been overlooked upon

as all that had happened

had wrecked her heart, and

numbed her mind

the endless tirade

had rummaged her bind

she could no longer relate

to the world around

she felt misplaced here

she felt UnBelonged.

The poem "Time is all we have and don't!" emphasizes the fleeting nature of time and the importance of cherishing the present moments.

Time is all we have and don't!

Time is all we have and don't
it's something we can never own.

The little moments that bring us joy,
we assume will always be there,
but once gone, they are lost forever,
never again to be found.

Spend an extra second, spend an extra minute,
appreciating all that you never did.
Spend an extra hour, spend an extra day,
living your wildest dreams in your own way.

For **time is all we have and don't**,
it keeps slipping away, we can never own.

The poem "Belonging to Eternity" contemplates the concept of time and the existence of the soul beyond the constraints of earthly life.

Belonging to Eternity

all our lives

we are made to believe

that we must live

to earn the goodwill

during our lifetime on earth

for the heavenly

afterlife experience

but it is not how it is

for there exists no time

there is only eternity, and

we are one soul changing forms

in the transient extraction

of timelessness

a combined amalgamation

of mass and energy

with an ad interim memory

moving with the universe

along with its ever-changing paradigms

We exist in the now, and

We exist in the then too.

FREEDOM

*Poems reflecting on personal liberation, breaking free
from constraints and embracing individuality.*

The poem "Unchained Thoughts" is a heartfelt expression of the longing to break free from the confines of emotional pain and embrace a life filled with love, joy and personal liberation.

Unchained Thoughts

I, no longer want to be enslaved,
in any grief of my wounded mind,
I want to seek my life, once again,
one that's free from all fiend.

I don't want my life to be a parody,
akin the soulless that you see everywhere,
I want my free spirit to leave footprints,
that will outlast me when I'm not there.

A world free of hurt and cacophony
is where I want to set my ground,
hearts overflowing with sublime love, and
floating mirth is what I want around.

In the depth of emotional wreckage,
I let loose all of my mind's despair,
unchaining my thoughts, I set them free,
to find their freedom again, in reverie.

The poem "Alis Volat Propriis" portrays the journey of a free-spirited individual breaking free from captivity and embracing their true nature by soaring and flying with their own wings.

Alis Volat Propriis

captivity was not meant for her

she was meant to fly

and, she did.

spreading her injured wings with pride

she took flight

to soar to the zenith

to touch the cerulean sky

to float amidst the clouds

to dance amongst the stars

to travel to the horizon, and

beyond

creating a trajectory of her own

releasing herself from all earthly binds

setting free her insecurities

she breathed her freedom

alis volat propriis

she flew with her own wings.

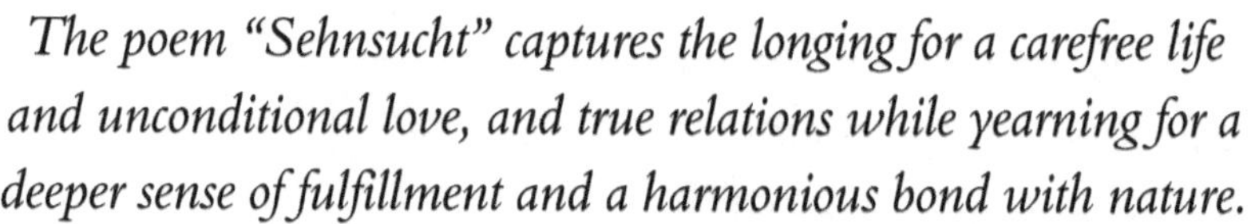

The poem "Sehnsucht" captures the longing for a carefree life and unconditional love, and true relations while yearning for a deeper sense of fulfillment and a harmonious bond with nature.

Sehnsucht

carefree life

raw innocence

unconditional love

dad's presence

real relations

recherchéd affections

freedom to live

in oneness with nature

without burning herself

for a secure future

the silent sighs exuded

her yearnings profound

each musing remained

a **sehnsucht** so long...

The poem "Ethereal Moments" is about the joy and enchantment that can be found in life's ethereal moments, and the reluctance to leave them behind and return to reality.

Ethereal Moments

On invisible wings against the winds

I take flight into the heavenly delight

with moments of enchantment adorning life

like the misty hues amidst the hazy white

drawing inspiration from the vast expanse

the universe rejoicing in an eternal dance.

Of halos and beauty that is rare

a miracle it is beyond compare

an echelon of stars that are glowing

in a deeper sense of bonding

and a growing sense of love

all woven together, to be held in awe.

Should I break this spell or let it be?

Should I fade back into the reality?

No.

I love these ethereal moments

they set me free

I do not want to be

pulled out from this reverie.

MEMOIR

Poems celebrating personal experiences, cherished memories, and transformative moments that shape the poet's journey.

The poem "Wanderer" is about a person who travels far and wide in search of peace, love, and answers in uncharted territories.

Wanderer

She traveled

far and wide

a sole wanderer

in quest of peace

across oceans, plateau, and

the jaded forests,

crossing deserts, planes, and

the mired valleys.

She traveled

far and wide

a sole wanderer

in search of love

the obscured sky above

the moonlit galaxy

besprinkled with stars

guiding her as a lighthouse.

She traveled

far and wide

a sole wanderer

in pursuit of answers,

through unknown paths

where no man had tread

keeping her will alive

in her sparkling eyes.

Unfazed by the outcome of ~

her quest, search and pursuit

bewildered by the realities

of the vagaries of life

imbuing the realms

like a wise sojourner

She traveled

far and wide

a sole wanderer.

The poem "Mirage" reflects on the idea of illusions and the feeling of being deceived by one's own vision.

Mirage

all that I

believed in

was but a dream

a carnival

a fanfare

or so it seemed.

I wanted

to capture

all that was

in my vision

I thought, I could

but 'twas my illusion.

the further I went

the farther it got

was it a horizon

or a mirage

that which

I sought?

I blinked my eyes

dream was gone

the mask torn

reality dawned

even before

my thought formed.

The poem "Life's path connects with me" reflects on the unpredictable and mysterious nature of life, the struggles of facing difficult moments, and the hope for a new beginning.

Life's Path Connects to Me ...

Strange is life, stranger are its ways,

filled as much with mystery as much as thrill,

when the shores are silent, the waves leave the bay,

like moments that seem as much alive as much as still.

The sun comes up, it's time to face the day

and, I think that life shall today be all right,

but, as the day wears on I don't let my nerves fray

to the hollowness that creeps within me every night.

Having reached crossroads at life, I'm feeling weary,

after the toils of sweat that over years I have shed.

and I'm feeling like the skies too are cloudy and dreary

like the emptiness within and the heart that has bled.

I know it's time to look ahead on the outside,

time to tread life's journey on a new way,

I'm wondering whether I'll ever find the strength inside,

to do it all again without going astray.

I have to erase the memories of how it began,

sift away the emotions from reality,

I wipe the mirror, dust on my hands,

the shadow clears, a new personality.

The wind blows a puff of scented fresh air,

I try to be tranquil, as much I can be

it lifts my spirits up, out of that dreaded despair,

sensing freedom above, I steer my life free.

I look to the sky, a cloudless sway

put a conch to my ear, a silent sea

strange is life, stranger are its ways,

an empty path ahead, that *connects to me.*

The poem "Lost Realm" explores the search for one's true self and the desire to break free from the confines of everyday life to find a realm of boundless potential.

Lost Realm

I feel at times,

I am not me.

Who can it be;

If I am not me?

I feel at times,

my realm, I seek.

If it isn't around me;

Where else can it be?

I feel at times,

I want to break free.

Am I so bound;

that I cannot break free?

As I seek to find

my true,

I walk under skies

gray and blue.

I see, I hear,

I touch, I feel,

I sift the unreal

from the real.

Boundless and bare,

lies my realm there.

Where fear is a myth

and hatred a rare.

The day I leave

all my pains behind

my true purpose in life

I will surely find.

The poem "Ashen Innocence" is about a person whose innocence was destroyed by the actions of others, leaving her with deep pain and sadness.

Ashen Innocence

A sparkle, a sunshine, a glowing light,
she came across as a harbinger of life.

Her spirit, her dreams were her pride,
she expressed it all with nothing to hide.

Tears of hurt often stream down her face,
as she reminisces of all that took place.

When the child within her left her side,
her careless whispers were buried inside.

She fought, she cried, she plead, she riled,
till all that was her soundlessly died.

What they did to her, consumed her soul,
her heart fragmented, will never be whole.

An epitome of innocence was reduced to ash,
such was her destiny that unfolded abashed.

The poem "My heart cries…" speaks of the deep pain and
sorrow felt by the daughter due to the loss of her father.

My Heart Cries...

There is so much pain that lies within my eyes,

but, alas, my eyes are dry,

I won't cry, for my eyes are dry,

No, I won't cry, for my eyes are dry...

The hope that once lived in my father's eyes has long been dead,

the heart that cared for everyone, to death has been bled.

When the cold wave came knocking to take my father astride,

the anguished soul of this daughter unseemingly died inside.

In the depth of solitude, the moments of togetherness glazed,

the footprints left in the sand, will with time be erased.

There was so much to be done and so much to be said,

unfulfilled will they remain, for my dear father is dead.

In his cherished and vivid memories, my heart bleeds,

for he was made to travel alone with all his good deeds.

The love that once lied within, will never surface again

for now all that has been left is pain, pain and pain.

Today, I feel the anger that burns within my gaze,

the cruelness of the incidents that has set my eyes ablaze,

the fear that in the darkness of the night closes my eyes,

the smile that I wear on my face is nothing but a disguise.

There is so much pain that lies within my eyes,

but, alas, my eyes are dry,

I won't cry for my eyes are dry,

No, I won't cry for my eyes are dry.

The poem "Fading Echoes" tells the story of a relationship marked by separations and reunions, where the protagonist holds onto hope despite the challenges they face.

Fading Echoes

When they first crossed their paths
they knew that they had given each other
a special place in their hearts
from strangers to friends, their journey was short
for their bonding was strong, right from the start.

He made her feel special and called her an angel
she helped him realize his dreams, and
gave him back his self-esteem
though they talked endlessly, they never met
yet, this was something they never regretted
till, one fine day...
when he disappeared from her life
without uttering any good byes
just as he had come he had gone away
leaving her wondering what led things astray
she cried and cried over the void he had left
she found no answers and moved on bereft.

Years passed and, again, one day...

he returned as if he had never gone away

she asked nothing and accepted him back, and

together they continued the journey of life

he set the child-woman in her free

all he craved for was her company

together, they dreamt new dreams, and

this time around, they promised to meet

but this was not how it was meant to be

such cruel was their destiny.

Time compelled them to travel different paths

even when they yearned for each other

they were forced to live, anonymously, apart

she did not know what to make of her strife

whether to accept him

as an anam cara or a traveler in her life

for what had happened once had recurred, again, and

deep in her heart she was numbed with pain

yet, she longed for him to come around

so, she kept her faith alive and her will strong

she prayed that when they meet again

which she hoped that they will

all that was there, would be there still...

The poem "Tears" is about the overwhelming pain and grief
that can leave a person feeling empty and trapped in their own
emotions.

Tears

as a tear drops from my eye

I feel the anguish deep inside

as it surges it harkens back in time

over the carefree moments, now lost

as a strange silence breaks my thoughts

abstract collages clutter my mind

I feel trapped within my own confines

in the reflections of darkness, I repine

I can't stop crying, I let them flow

for my grief-stricken heart is hollow

I know something within me has died

that I am feeling empty, I can't hide

I can't count my wounds, they are too many

I need solace but can't find any.

all I feel is hurt, all I sense is pain,

all that remains are my tears, an echoing refrain.

The poem "Silence to Resilience" reflects on the ups and downs of life, from innocence to maturity, and the journey towards resilience.

Silence to Resilience

As I pondered in silence...

my life reeled before me

from when I had my sensibilities

a myriad of collages, replayed

some clear, some cluttered,

yet, somehow, they all mattered.

A journey indeed it's been for me,

from innocence to maturity

melancholy to serendipity

seen it all, done it all, and

learnt from every climb and fall

there were the lows and the highs

ensembled with the worldly sighs.

Awed, stricken, diffident and disdained

every emotion within me has been raked

been a wreck when filled with void

but have also experienced sheer pride

bouncing back has been a pattern of my life

through every crisis, windfall and strife.

Destiny's favorite child, that is me ~

I have accepted it now and set myself free,

in the depth of silence, I found the key,

resilience, it shall be till eternity.

The poem "Child of Destiny" portrays the soul as a divine creation destined for a unique and significant purpose in the realm of existence.

Child of Destiny

an expression of love

filled with mirth

a seed of human

birthed on earth

an epitome of beauty

chaste, rare

a paragon of history

mystical faire

an alchemic artistry

of the almighty

a true child of destiny

was she

The poem "Journey-In" explores the inner turmoil and subsequent self-discovery as the author delves into the depths of her chaotic mind, uncovering a free spirit.

Journey-In...

pandemonium inundated

my chaotic mind

not knowing

where to dive

I plunged inside

a tunneled inroad

that's how it seemed

feelings interspersed

in layers deep

as I unraveled

I was touched by

what I unearthed

a free spirit that

danced in mirth

enchanted with all

the kosher love-in

thus, began

my *journey-in...*

TRIBUTE

Poems paying homage to womanhood and cherished relationships.

The poem "Beauty of a Woman" celebrates the inner and outer grace of a woman, highlighting her ability to bring joy, wisdom, and love to the world.

Beauty of a Woman

She walks with elegance, poise and grace,
her aura pure, untouched by worldly chase.
Her beauty lies not in cosmetics trace,
nor in adorned attire, a fleeting embrace.

Her soft eyes hold wisdom, gentle and kind,
thoughts eloquent, soothing troubled minds.
Her presence brings light, darkness unwinds,
transforming shadows, radiant hope finds.

She connects souls, with care and delight,
weaving joy serenely, embracing the night.
An embodiment of love, a purest sight,
a blessing from above, shining ever bright.

Woman – You are LIFE.

The poem "She" portrays the depth and complexity of a woman's identity, celebrating her as a unique and powerful entity within the larger universe.

She

a universe exists within her

a mélange of stars

a tsunami of waves

a parched desert

a wild jungle

an amazing creation

by the creator

she is an embodiment of

protection

purity, and

power

she is the whole

inside the whole

an infinite realm

with a soul.

The poem "Dad – My first Love, My forever Hero" reflects on the deep love and admiration for a father, expressing the longing for his presence, the brokenness of heart after his loss, and the hope of meeting again in the afterlife, while keeping his memory alive in the meantime.

Dad
My First Love, My Forever Hero

Dad...

my first LOVE,

my forever HERO.

be it laughter, happiness

sunshine, rain

without you besides

they never feel the same

my heart is broken

this ain't a lie

all I feel

are the remorseful sighs

wanting to

see you once more

cuddle you with love

hear you call me

touch you somehow.

I was the luckiest

to have had

the world's best dad

belong to me

how, I wish this

could be true

for eternity.

though the journey is onerous

there is hope guiding the way

that we will meet once again

when I reach the pearly gates.

till, then...

I remain confined

in your shrine

while keeping your flame

burning inside mine.

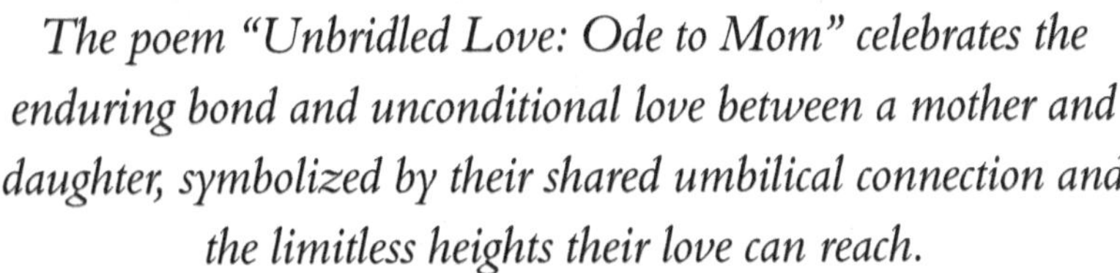

The poem "Unbridled Love: Ode to Mom" celebrates the enduring bond and unconditional love between a mother and daughter, symbolized by their shared umbilical connection and the limitless heights their love can reach.

Unbridled Love: Ode to Mom

Mom, you are the beacon that guides my way,
in this ode, I honor you today.

Our bond, unwavering, like no other,
a connection forged by our shared umbilical tether.

Through life's journey, you have been my steadfast guide,
in your embrace, I find solace and abide.

Your love knows no bounds, a flame that forever burns,
nurturing my dreams, each step of the way it churns.

In your presence, I am wrapped in warmth and care,
an emotion so pure, beyond words we share.

You have shaped my world, your love deeply known,
a bond unbridled, forever grown.

REFLECTION

Poems imploring introspection, self-discovery and contemplation of life's deeper truths.

The poem "Circle of Life" reflects on the journey from conception to death, highlighting the experiences, choices, and growth that shape our path, and embracing the cyclical nature of life.

Circle of Life

Born from love's tender embrace,

within the womb's protective grace,

we embark on life's unfolding quest,

with hope, faith and trials to test.

Our choices shape the path we tread,

through moments high and low, we are led,

creating, passing life's sacred thread,

hoping they find their own light spread.

Guided by change, we discover our might,

unveiling dimensions once hidden from sight,

living life fully, embracing the fight,

until we embrace the end, embracing the night.

Like nature's seasons in circle's flow,

life's mysteries unfold for us to explore,

in the eternal journey we undertake,

The Circle of Life, aglow.

The poem "Ignis Aurum Probat" explores the enduring purity and resilience of an individual as they navigate through the complexities and trials of life, symbolized by the Latin phrase "Ignis aurum probat."

Ignis Aurum Probat

Here and there, in reality and dreams
lay her life, pristine and threadbare
altering with the seasons of time
as she moved on time after time after time.

the eloquence of her simplicity
stood out amidst the guiled masks
masquerading everywhere
undeterred she remained
as she paved through
the complexities and trials
that inquisitioned
her fortitude in her quest
she kept combing through the labyrinth
through signs known and unknown
to seek the eternal truth
her endurance absolute.

Ignis aurum probat

refined after being tested in fire

her sacred sanctity unscathed

she radiated her inner purified light.

The poem "Observer and I" explores the internal struggle of a person who seeks understanding and knowledge but feels limited by the complexities and uncertainties of the world.

Observer and I

She sits alone

watching a world of her own

appearing lost but she is not

she wants to understand

and know much more

which when her 'she' is 'I'

she cannot know.

The order, the light

amidst the chaos and fright

the unsolicited incite

that deflect her might

the illusory contours

that keep her ashore

the obscure metaphors

that chain her to her yore

the twisted crossroads

that debilitate her will

the monochromes, the shadows

that hold her still.

it is when she is plagued with so many 'why's'

that she lets the 'Observer' in her become the 'I'.

The poem "Tabula Rasa" portrays a journey of overcoming darkness and starting anew with a clean slate, propelled by hope and the desire to create a fulfilling life.

Tabula Rasa

Memories, vivid yet distant

of how colors turned gray

in the contours of her convoluted mind

over the years, it seemed like

there could be nothing more

to the black hole-like darkness

that shrouded her vision

gripping her imagery

she sat there lost

in the qualms of her fragmented life.

Interlude

She could not let this continue

it had to stop

for she was breathing, she was alive

and deep within she knew

it was temporary

she had to move on in life.

Interlude

She woke up one day
and set her slate clean
like the tabula rasa
and edged forward, propelled with hope
towards the horizon
ready to create new imprints
of the rest of her life.

The poem "In the Stillness..." is a contemplative reflection on finding liberation and self-discovery within the tranquil depths of one's mind.

In the Stillness…

In the stillness of my mind,

I saw myself unchained, unbound.

In the whispers of my heart,

I found my voice.

In the trajectory of my dreams,

I made my choice.

In the realm of my soul,

I sought peace.

In the depths of my being,

I believed.

For in the stillness of my mind,

I was unchained, unbound,

A celebration of liberation, resound.

The poem "Reflect" explores the act of pausing and observing one's life, acknowledging the diverse and colorful experiences that shape who we are.

Reflect

I pause at times
to see my state
in a new light
when my canvas is
overflowing with the
colors of life
not, all are
the brights, and
the hues
some are shaded
with grays, too
but as the
drops of colors
burst to form shapes
I feel, a feel
that is strange yet true
that they are
a vivid expression
of all that I do, and
the choices that I make
as life passes through.

The poem "Stringing the Unstrung" portrays the power of a weaver who brings harmony and purpose to the chaotic threads of life, weaving together tales of hope and resilience.

Stringing the Unstrung

In the realm of chaos, where disarray is rife,

a weaver emerges, to bring harmony to life.

She spins tales of hope, resilience, and dreams,

stringing the unstrung, with vibrant seams.

With every untangled note, a story unfolds,

the symphony of life, in her hands it molds.

She weaves together emotions, joy and despair,

creating a fusion of melodies rare.

Silent whispers, now find their song,

as the unstrung find purpose, where they belong.

The poem "Sometimes That, Sometimes This" portrays a soul's journey in pursuit of love, peace, untrodden paths and enlightenment, dancing with simplicity and bliss.

Sometimes That, Sometimes This...

a soul, seeking
hoping and yearning

a heart, longing for
love and peace

a traveler, in quest of
untread paths and fresh air

a seeker, pursuing
answers and light

she was beautifully out of place
she was magically blended in it

she was sometimes that
she was sometimes this

a palpable spirit who danced in abandon
filled with simplicity and bliss.

The poem "When I Go" depicts a soul's message to loved ones, urging them not to grieve but to find solace in the understanding that the soul has merged harmoniously with nature after departing from its physical form.

When I Go...

When it's time, and

I fly off

into the

prismatic yonder

do not cry for me here

for here is not

where I will be

I may blend-in

with the gaia, aurora

or briny sea

whatever be

my transcension

know that

I did not die

I just winged away

with palpable

unbridled mirth

and, joy.

End Note

To all the readers of *Inkspiration: A Collection of Poetic Musings*, I extend my deepest gratitude. It is my hope that these poems have touched your soul, providing solace, inspiration and a connection to the shared human experience.

As I pen these closing words, my heart brims with gratitude for the voyage we have undertaken together. Through the medium of poetry, we have explored the expansive realm of emotions, delved into introspection and found solace in the captivating beauty of language. Thank you for allowing my words to resonate within you.

May the echoes of these poems continuously reverberate in your heart, serving as a reminder of the timeless allure and transformative power of the written word. THANK YOU for being a cherished reader on this poetic odyssey.

With genuine appreciation,

Aishwarya Damodar